The Guide For 1st G

NOW WHAT?!

COACH T'S GUIDE FOR 1ST GENERATION

COLLEGE STUDENTS & THEIR PARENTS

TaNesha "Coach T" McAuley

CONTENTS

Introduction To You the Future College Student: 3

Chapter 1 What's The Big Deal About College? 8

Chapter 2 I Want To Attend College! Now What? 17

Chapter 3 You've Been Accepted Into A College! Now What? 30

Chapter 4 Conquering the Freshman Fears. How? 41

Chapter 5 Selecting A Major. How?! 52

Chapter 6 Managing Your Independence As A College Student. How?! 62

Chapter 7 Pledging. What's The Big Deal about Greek Life?! 93

Chapter 8 What's Really Real About The "Real World"? 101

Chapter 9 You Did It! (Graduation) Now What? 108

Chapter 10 Your First Career Interview After Graduation! Now What?! 112

Chapter 11 Living Your Best Life? You Already Are! 120

Scholarships.com Links 127

Acknowledgments 129

INTRODUCTION

To You the Future College Student:

I am thrilled to release this manual to you, the first-time college student, and your parent(s) who may not have a true grasp of college experience. Through my research and experience, I learned that we're known as 1st Generation students or 1st Gen's for short. We're the ones who became the first, within our immediate and sometimes extended family, to attend college. There was no one in our family that could give us insight on how to prepare or what to expect. Everything we learned about college was through school and our peers.

I was compelled to write this manual because my experience with college was a rollercoaster. It was NOTHING like high school. You're technically thrown into adulthood and independence without a complete understanding of what to expect. Neither my mother nor I had a clue on where to begin. Prior to considering college, I was strongly considering the Army after graduation. My mom was completely opposed to that idea, but I was determined to enroll considering I had spent 4 years in JROTC and had worked my way up to being Company Commander. I don't know what changed my mind. Maybe it was the prayers of my mother or maybe it was fate that I decided to pursue college. When I made up my mind to do so, I was behind the 8-ball significantly. When I talked with my school guidance counselor, I was told about community college options. I didn't know anything about application processes, having GPA scores to increase my chances of getting accepted, how to pay for college, scholarships, and so much more. Anything that I did learn about the college processes was through my peers and I knew that I needed more information than that.

After successfully navigating the college scene and earning my undergraduate and graduate degrees, I vowed that I would offer something to other students, who are just like me, concerning college. Clueless with no one to give them an understanding on the in's and out's. If someone had offered me a guide or manual, I probably would have had a much easier transition. It probably would have helped my mom too because she didn't know what to expect either. The core of what I do remember were the feelings of fear, confusion, frustration, excitement, and anticipation.

While your college experience will be different from mine, this guide serves as a foundation of some commonalities that you will have. There are just some things that every college student will have to do and as a 1st Gen, I want to give the gift of doing it as best as possible the first go round in order to avoid some of the pitfalls I and countless of others have made. If you don't remember anything else from this manual, remember this; make sure that college is what you want to do and that you're enrolling for the right reasons. If you have absolutely no desire to attend college, then don't. Don't fall under the pressure from family and friends. Maybe you feel you need some time after you graduate from high school. If that's the case, then trust your gut. Be open in your communication about what YOU desire to do as it relates to college. If you do decide that college is for you, understand that it will be challenging in the beginning but you can make it. You will survive. Be consistent. Be resilient.

To the Parent,

Sending your first baby off to college can be scary. You're uncertain if they can handle it. If they will be okay. How they'll adjust. You'll probably struggle with your youth being away from home and there may be a small part of you that will want to discourage them to attend college. I recall my mom sharing how hard it was for her to accept that I was leaving for college. Although we would only be 1-hour in distance, she still struggled. Guess what? We got through it and so will you and your teen. After I completed my first year, my mother and I were smooth sailing. We still had some bumps in the road but we navigated them well enough. We got connected with some really great resources that were able to help me through the process. I met some really great friends with loving parents that treated me as their own. I never went without food. I didn't get involved in hard-core drugs or other reckless behavior outside of the "normal" college stuff like staying out late partying, eating unhealthy foods, and consuming alcohol while underage. You and your youth will be just fine. I suggest establishing times to visit and stay connected and as the parent, trust your gut when something feels off. Make the call. Make the trip. Stay connected and involved. There are so many opportunities on college campus to keep families and their college student connected and engaged in the process. Now What?!

CHAPTER 1

What's The Big Deal About College?

College is about campus life, dorm room living, roommates, socializing, partying, attending classes, professors, fraternities, sororities, guys, girls, relationships, dating, break ups, sports, and did I mention studying, left-brain learning, exams, first semesters, financial aid, books, long nights, bad eating and much more? While college encompasses a lot of great things, there are some things that the college experience doesn't teach you and that's about the real world during and after graduating college. When I say the "real" world, I'm referring to how students should apply all of their knowledge that they obtain in college in practical settings. In all fairness to college professors, teaching the basics of academia is enough within itself, so it's hardly enough time to devote classes or studies on how college students can manage their finances, their physical and mental health, nutrition, how to prepare for job interviews, how to negotiate your first salary, how to design your resume to align with the jobs you are applying to, or just the basic life skills to living. Students and parents often assume that because you have a degree, you're set for life, right? Unfortunately, many college graduates are not as prepared as they could, or should be, when they walk across the stage. They are sometimes or oftentimes unprepared for the "real" world such as knowing how to be prepared for your first professional job interview, knowing how to dress appropriately for the interview, managing a budget that doesn't involve assistance from grants, scholarships, and loans, figuring out where to start applying for jobs once you've gotten your degree, and so much more.

So, who is this guide for? It's for you, your sibling(s) when they head off to college, your parents, or anyone who wants to do college in the most practical and sensible way without too many bumps and bruises. Being the first one in your family to attend college, you may not have the best idea of what to expect from the time you start to the time you finish. I won't even get started about all of the navigating in between, and how to stay afloat when you feel like quitting or giving up. You see, it's students like me that heard everyone talking about how great it was to attend college and how if you didn't attend, you'd pretty much be a bum in your parent's home until you were a full fledged adult; working in your local Waffle House and running into people you graduated high school with. Sound pretty accurate? If so, keep reading. I originally started offering this information on college campuses to universities that would invite me in to speak to students about being prepared for the real world. Let's be honest. Colleges do a great job preparing you for the major you're interested in pursuing, and they do a swell job in helping you become acclimated to the college experience like homecoming, pep rallies, concerts, step shows, band performances, games, and so much more; however, unless you are intentional about taking courses that specifically teach you about life, you're joining the ranks in learning the quick and dirty way about life and independence after college is completed. Don't get me wrong; I survived, and many others have as well, but why not provide some insight to future generations on how to navigate or potentially avoid some of the same pitfalls?

What's the big deal about college? So here it goes. This is for the parents. Please! During your urging of your high school graduate about college enrollment, be sure to ask IF they want to attend college and WHY. From my own personal experience, making a flip decision to attend college, without vetting the process, can leave your young one riddled in a world of debt of student loans, a major in a potential field that wouldn't even get them a job at most fast food restaurants, wasted time, wasted energy, and much more. I'll be the first to acknowledge that it is truly a blessing and it is very exciting when you have a daughter or son that could be the first one in the family to attend college. It's a great feeling when you get the opportunity to see the fruits of your labor and have bragging rights amongst your friends at work and church, on how your kid was accepted into so and so college. I get it. However, it's worthy to support your child through the process of determining if college is for them or if college is for them immediately after graduating high school. I know it's scary to think about them being home for the summer and not going off to school like some of their peers. I know it's even scarier to think they don't have a life plan and will probably eat you out of a house and a home. Better yet, I know it's frightening to think about them becoming another local statistic, but would you rather know what their true abilities and plans were before pushing them onto a path that may not be designed for them? Research found that in 2016, more than 48% of first-time full-time students, who started at a four-year college six years earlier, had not yet earned a degree. For these universities, the four-year completion rate is just 28%. Stated in another way, nearly 2 million students, who begin college each year, will drop out before earning a bachelors degree. The picture is no different at local community colleges, with only 26% of full-time students completing their degree. This is not to discourage you as the parent nor student, but it is to help you and your future student make the best choice possible when it comes to college enrollment. Well, how will I know if college is for me you may ask? How will I know if college is for my child? Here are some key points to consider on both sides:

- Have you, as the high school graduate, ever said you wanted to attend college outside of the reason "that's what all of my friends are doing?"

- What was their motivation like in high school? Did they barely make it? Was maintaining a C average a struggle?

- To the parent: Has your graduate told you that they do not want to attend college?

- Are they creative and tend to thrive better in a creative space; i.e. interest in the arts, crafts, designing, building, creating, bringing their imaginations to life, etc.?

- To the student: Did you put in the proper planning to go on college tours?

- Did you have meetings with your guidance counselor, or others that had attended college, that could give you some practical insight?

Now, this is a very miniscule assessment and by far doesn't denote someone shouldn't attend college; however, it's a good baseline to determine next steps in the process. If I had to pick one out of the bunch, I would certainly pay attention to the bullet point where the student has stated they are not interested in attending. This is a great measuring tool before trudging along into filling out college applications and spending unnecessary application fees. If your kid is saying they don't want to attend college, the next best thing you can do, as a parent, is to support their decision and ask questions that will provoke sound thought and reason as to why they don't want to. Trust me, even if it's because they're lazy and don't do much of anything but sit around, you do not want to lock horns on this one because they'll only get into college and be lazy, sit around and do much of nothing. Which one would you rather experience?

I'll say it for you. "The lazy person at home instead of the lazy person at college." "Why?" Because college is too expensive to pay $4k or more, per year, for someone to just sit around and do much of nothing. As I'm sure you've heard, and I will reiterate; college is NOT for everyone. There; I said it. I know it can be a tough pill to swallow but I promise, this will save you and your youth the headache, hassle, and money you would throw away. It's best for you and your teen to explore all of the options available that can help develop them academically, socially, mentally, and financially.

CHAPTER 2

I Want To Attend College! Now What?

You've decided to go to college, so what's next? There is a lot that goes into planning for a college education well before your teen starts the application and enrollment process, and that's preparing financially. As a parent, you may have already established the income and funds necessary for college but if there are opportunities for scholarships and grants, why not take advantage of it? As 1st Gen students, there are some really unique and specific funding that you can apply for and receive that will aid your teen financially in college. I wish I had known this information when I was in high school. It was so easy to get caught in the loop of conversations about attending college but not having a clear path on how to make it a reality. As someone who didn't understand the process, I just assumed that money would fall from the sky or that college would be paid for. Boy, I was wrong! You must be intentional about planning for college and the financial obligations that comes with it. I remember sitting in the crowd with my class on graduation day and hearing many of my classmate's names being called out and being recognized for scholarships they had received. I had no clue of what was going on or how they got scholarships and I didn't. I figured it was only for athletic or academic achievements they had made while in school. *Maybe these scholarships were only for straight "A" students* I thought. I never knew there were scholarships that you could apply for even if you hadn't gotten into a specific college. These were literally scholarships that you could apply for based off of various factors and meeting the requirements from the scholarship donor. I heard about scholarships obviously, but I didn't know the first step to begin applying for, or better yet, researching and finding where scholarships were hiding out. I didn't know that my school guidance counselor could help me seek out and explore scholarship opportunities. I didn't know that scholarships could range in different amounts. I didn't know that you could qualify for scholarships based off of your family makeup such as living in a single-parent household or that there were income contingent scholarships if your household made a certain amount of income. So, in order for you and your teen to avoid this pitfall, it's important to begin the research and the process as early as possible. Some scholarship opportunities are not available until senior year of high school but there may be prerequisites (preconditions, fundamentals) that have to be met prior to enrollment. These generations have way more advantages than we did years ago such as advanced technology of the

Internet, YouTube, social media, and so much more. When I finally learned the available scholarships and how to apply for them, it was through a pamphlet that listed out various scholarships from various donors and companies, and the steps to apply.

Below are a list of steps that you and your teen can take to get ahead of locating and applying for scholarship offers before college enrollment:

- Use the Internet and search for local scholarships first. These are oftentimes untapped resources because we tend to think large is the only size of money when it comes to scholarships.
- Research local faith-based organizations, especially if you're a part of a church or other religious sector.

- Despise not small beginnings. Meaning…do not turn down or turn up your nose at small scholarship and grant awards. I've seen scholarships as small as $25-50 and they came in extremely handy. These amounts can add up and support you with food, dorm room supplies, books, and other miscellaneous expenses.

- Search local, county, state, and federal websites in search engines with the term "scholarship dollars", "college grants", along with the year.

- For 1st Gen students, there are specific scholarships and grant dollars that your teen can qualify for.

- Search in advance to determine what the qualifications are. Most scholarship awards are attached to your academic or athletic performance in school. You will need to ensure that you work to maintain a good GPA, and it will also be ideal if you get involved in school organizations. There are key scholarships and grants attainable with a solid and strong academic record.

- If your teen is an athlete, there are additional scholarship options on the table.

- Later in the manual, I will have a list of scholarship links that you can add to your menu.

While you're searching scholarship and grant offers, it's important to begin exploring schools of interest to determine what the tuition and fees will be. I have to be transparent again and admit that I had NEVER done this nor had my mom. We were clueless to look at the cost of attendance to a four-year college. We just knew that I had to apply, wait for an acceptance letter, and show up. That's pretty much what happened. I was fortunate in the absence of knowledge and blessed in the midst of naivety. My school of attendance was in-state and tuition was $4k per year, and that didn't include books. I was ill prepared financially for the transition from high school to college. I was going along as though I would show up the same way to college as I did for high school, with everything being provided for me. Boy, I was sadly mistaken. These are a few tips to consider when looking at the cost of tuition:

- What would a monthly or annual payment look like if there weren't any scholarships or grants secured?

- Are you in a position financially to pay this bill if there weren't any scholarship money?

- Are there resources, through your employer, that offers tuition assistance for college for your teen?

- If your teen doesn't receive a full scholarship to cover their college costs, what types of financial support will you need to include loans?

- Will you be able to get a loan in your name if your teen is not approved for a full loan amount in their first year?

- Review student loan repayment plans for different types of educational loans such as Stafford Direct Student loans, Sallie Mae, subsidized and unsubsidized loans. This will help prepare you and your teen in case you have to apply for a loan and you're not caught off guard when you have to complete all of the paperwork.

- Compare the cost of tuition between similar schools of interest. Look for colleges that offer programs that your teen is interested in. This may be a little challenging because most majors aren't declared until late sophomore to early junior year. Don't let that discourage you from doing the homework to gain as much clarity possible.

- Consider bank loans if you're more interested in repayment plans that starts before graduating from college. This option lessens the amount of interest that will accumulate on student loans.

After you've done the groundwork for identifying funding for college, the next conversation will probably be on housing. As a 1st Gen student, the thought of living anywhere outside of campus never crossed my mind. For one, I didn't know it was an option, and two, because I had never lived independent of my parents. This would have been another huge adjustment that I would not have been ready for. My advice to students and parents is to strongly consider on-campus housing. I recommend this for various reasons which include; living on campus gives the student the opportunity to adjust to the campus life. They get the chance to meet and learn about people outside of their normal circle and surroundings, and also become acclimated with what college is really about. I had several friends that tried off-campus housing and they failed tremendously as a result of having to work in order to pay rent, drive to class, and find parking in time before class started. Campus parking was horrible then and I'm sure it's worse now. Trying to make it to class through morning or evening traffic is a headache and it adds more pressure on the student that's trying to commute from home to class.

Now, I'm sure this places a damper on your youth who has ideas of living a lavish life in this super posh apartment with their friends and feels like this is the first taste of freedom that they'll have. I promise. They will have a lot of time to be independent and pay bills, and will be amazed at how much independence living on campus will offer. In addition to independence, it offers a great deal of support which leads to accountability. When you hear the stories on how people met some of their closest and best friends on college, that was all truth and I believe everyone that has attended college has had this experience. When I first arrived to college, I only knew two people from my hometown that was enrolled at the time, and I knew two of my high school classmates that were attending. When I arrived at my dormitory, I went to my room assignment at which time, I met my roommate. She was super friendly but her mother was a little standoffish, catching me by surprise. I'm sure my daisy "dukes" and midriff top was a little off-putting and probably gave the impression that I would be a bad influence. After getting my belongings settled in, I recall sitting on my bed trying to figure out the next thing to do; where to go eat, how to get to the cafeteria, how would I figure out my classes and so many other things that I didn't know about. It was only then a brave young girl on our hallway, Kovi, decided to walk down to our room, introduce herself and her roommate, and invite us down to meet other hall mates. This was officially the beginning of building friendships with other girls that I still remain great friends with today, in 2019. Is this everyone's experience? Of course not, however, I have heard more similar experiences like mine versus not. The only way I would recommend off-campus housing would be if on-campus housing weren't available. Living on campus was extremely beneficial during in climate weather, like the year we experienced the worst snowstorm in history. Although classes had been cancelled, the cafeteria remained open and we were able to walk to get food. We also kept our electricity whereas residential areas had lost power for weeks. Other complaints that I heard about off-campus living was the wait time between classes and not having anywhere to go outside of the library or the yard if you didn't have friends in the dorm. On long days, you could easily have a 45-minute to 1-hour break before your next class and for most college students, the first thought was to go back to your room and catch a quick nap. If the decision is to go the off-campus route, please consider the following:

- Ensure that you're within a close distance from campus to avoid traffic congestion, morning commute accidents, and so forth while driving to school.

- Live in an area that has public transportation to alleviate the drive.

- Understand that this is not ideal for students that are not morning people and waking up early is their worst enemy. Most freshman class schedules are mostly in the morning with the earliest class starting at 8:00 or 8:30 AM.

- Invest in parking passes and decals. Do not try to pass go without making this investment. A lot of students would try to locate street parking or other areas to avoid paying for parking and a lot of students were met with tickets and boots being placed on their vehicles.

- Make friends with student's on-campus so that when you have a long break between classes and don't want to drive home, you can crash at their dorm room.

CHAPTER 3

You've Been Accepted Into A College! Now What?

Congratulations! I'm sure you and your family are excited that you've been accepted into college. You may have even gotten several offers and unsure of where to go. If that's the case, I would suggest that you "pro-con" the colleges to determine which university is going to suit your needs best. These are things to take into consideration once you've gotten your acceptance letter from several different colleges:

- If you have time or the ability, based on the location, go onto the campus and tour it without the pressure of being with your high school peers. Sometimes, college tours seemed more fun when we did them with our friends. They would put on these great performances to entice young minds to attend their university. It's best to visit the potential college without all the bells and whistles so that you can make an unbiased decision. It's best to focus on the college's graduation rate and how successful they are with the programs they offer to students.

- Look at the numbers and compare cost between the offers. If two or more of the colleges you're interested in have similar backgrounds, consider the cost of tuition and allow this to help in making your choice from a cost-savings standpoint.

- Follow your heart. At the end of the day, your youth is the individual that will be attending and will need to connect with the institution they believe will best meet and serve their needs.

Now that you've selected your school of choice, these are the things that you must begin planning for in case no one told you; like no one told me:

- Furnishing and accessories for your dorm room. You'll need bedding and accessories to make your room comfortable because this is where you'll spend a lot of time.

- Find out if you'll have to supply your own fridge or if one will come inside of your dorm room. It's best to have your very own and not depend on the university providing this type of amenity.

- Toiletries because colleges do not provide these things. Unfortunately, colleges aren't the Hilton hotels. If you have a shared space, you'll probably have to share a bathroom. In this case, you'll want to invest in great shower shoes (shoes you only wear in the shower). This may sound like a no-brainer but several girls in my dorm took their first dorm shower barefooted. Yeah, it's gross and that's one experience you want to avoid at all cost.

- Start a bank account with at least $100-500 to float you until your scholarship money or loans kick in. Start saving from your part-time income at Burger King or Mickey D's or wherever you are employed. Trust me, this is imperative because I wasn't aware that I had to pay for books out of my pocket, and that the amount would be in the tune of about $500-800 dollars. This was only for books in the first semester.

- If you're planning to drive to school, first, you'll need to review your school's policy for freshman drivers. Some universities prohibit first-year drivers. This is primarily done to cut down on overcrowding and parking congestion. In hindsight, it also serves as a way to ensure new students don't get too distracted with that level of freedom and interfere with attendance. If you are permitted to drive, you'll need to ensure proper insurance and registration, and proper parking decals.

- Find out about all of the technology you'll need to complete assignments. Laptop and computers are another luxury that's not provided by your academic institution (at least not some)

[

- Make sure you know your dorm assignment as far ahead as possible. This should be resolved by attending freshman orientation. Please attend this event. This was another area that I didn't have a clue about and realized this was how some of the groups and friendships were formed even before starting classes.

- Meet and build a rapport with your Residential Assistant (RA). They will be able to assist with a lot of questions you'll have.

- Tour the campus to ensure you know your class schedule and the buildings your class will be in. Also, make sure you know where the gym and cafeteria are located. There will always be students hanging out in these two areas.

Once you've gotten your dorm assignment, you will have to meet with your Academic Advisor in order to enroll in your classes. Each college will have a different process, so make sure you know your school's process. When all else fails, ask questions and get clarity. If you're required to take any placement test, this will happen first to ensure you're prepared for the classes you enroll in. Your Advisor will also ensure you understand the amount of hours you can enroll in for each semester. I advise to start with no more than 15 hours. It's important to adjust first and then on your second year, add more if you think you're capable. I'll insert this for reality; you should explore having fun while you're in college. Learn how to balance fun and school work if you want to be successful at having good grades and graduating. It's no point in overwhelming yourself with taking a huge load of hours in the beginning. You'll have more than enough time to be progressive with your classes. Also, as a form of encouragement, please do not feel like you have to be in the rat race with the individuals that decide to complete their four-year program in 3 years. As a seasoned college graduate and professional, I have a hard time understanding why students place this type of pressure on themselves. I get it. It sounds really smart and adult-like when people say they're finishing school in 3 years but after that, what else? Will finishing a year earlier get you a head start in your profession? Will it be more impressive on your resume? I can answer honestly and say "NO".

After getting enrolled in classes, you'll meet with your financial aid advisor if you have to go the route of getting a student loan. You will, or at least, should be advised about the amount you'll be signing up for and how much of your loans, grants, and scholarships will cover your classes, and if anything will be left over to pay for books. The most important piece of advice I can offer on this subject is to compare cost of books with discount bookstores and other sellers. And don't be afraid or too proud to invest in used books. It will save you tons of money. The scariest and most depressing moment for me was when I realized that I needed to pay for books and I didn't have enough financial aid to cover them. My mother had to apply for a Parent Plus loan to get me the money. This is the main reason why I recommend having a banking account with at least $100-500 or more saved for these types of emergencies. I was so glad that my mother was able to meet the qualifications for getting the loan, but it also created another bill for her. I was so oblivious to the beginning experiences that I briefly dealt with minor depression. How could I get through school AND survive all of the requirements. I became even more depressed when I heard other students talking about refund checks and how they were getting thousands of dollars back to shop with. How did that happen? They were informed and were knowledgeable about the process.

Another piece of advice I would offer is that if you're considering maintaining a summer job or wanting to work while you're in college, only do so on the weekends because you really don't want work to interfere with your college experience and you don't want to overload yourself as you make this new transition. It's so easy to get caught in the flow of everyone else's plans and forget what your needs and goals are. If you don't read anything else in this manual, highlight this statement:

BE GENTLE WITH YOURSELF

You will have more than enough time to figure it all out and the great thing is that, you don't have to do it alone. It will be very tempting to start working to earn extra money to purchase the latest fashion and technology. With this in mind, you must avoid the credit card trap that has gotten a lot of students in bad debt. You are an easy target and extremely attractive to creditors that know you'll be irresponsible and rack up loads of debt by charging everything instead of paying cash. While having a credit card for emergencies can be good, having one just to spend unnecessarily is not. During my first tour of my college campus, there were credit card tables and representatives set up near the Student Union as a way to entice students to apply. Naturally, you'll get approved and probably have a very high interest rate, so if you decide to use it, you technically pay more for the item than what it's valued at. If you do decide to use a credit card, here are a few tips that will keep you out of the red zone:

- Never max out your card

- Always pay your balance in full. Only charge what you're able to pay off before the next billing cycle.

- Only get one credit card. Stay away from retail credit cards. Those interest rates are OUTRAGEOUS!

- Never allow friends or family to use or make purchases with your credit card. This is a huge NO-NO.

- Research to see which credit cards offer you best rates and reward points. Some of the reward programs can be used to get discounts from your favorite or most shopped stores, gas, grocery, and many other perks.

- If you don't have to use your card, don't. Keep it for emergencies or rainy days.

CHAPTER 4

Conquering the Freshman Fears.
How?

You've survived getting enrolled in classes, standing in lines for financial aid, getting your dorm assignment, paying for all of your books, navigating the campus and not getting lost, meeting and making new friends, sleeping in a foreign place, and much more and now, you have started your first week of school. Having fun yet? The first week of class can, and will, be draining considering all of the things you had to do up unto that point. You've met your professors; you've realized that college is nothing like high school, and you've probably realized that this is part of the independence you've craved for. The professors probably gave you a syllabus for the semester that included a reading assignment on your first day as though their class is the only class you enrolled in right? Brace yourself because the overwhelm will set in really quickly. You'll start to miss home and the comforts of your "normal" life. After my first or maybe second week of college, I called my mom "boo-hoo" crying, saying I wanted to leave college and return home. I was so distraught and my home was only one measly hour away from college! There were some of my classmates that went to college out of state so I couldn't even begin to imagine their level of homesickness. I cried and cried that I wanted to come home and she almost bought it until a close family friend warned her of the damage and ramifications that could ensue if she allowed me to walk away. Boy, was I glad for that advice? I needed to remain enrolled in order to see how resilient I really was and to learn how to work through the discomforts of life. You'll need to do the same. Remember the discouraging statistics from earlier in the read about how many percentage of 1st Gen students drop out from college in the first year? I didn't want to be a statistic. Here are a few tips to avoid the homesick/"I want to go home" feeling:

- Stay connected with family and friends back home through the use of technology. If I had access to today's technology back when I was in college, things would have been a little better. With FaceTime, Skype, and other video chat options, you can see and talk with family and friends that are far away.

- Get active with your new buddies in your dorm. Find the ones that you connect with and put your energy into building strong foundations. As a disclaimer, everyone will not like you or want to be friends with you.

The ones who do, you will connect with and the ones that don't, they will keep it moving.

- Talk about your emotions and feelings with people who can help you put things into perspective and encourage you to stay course. The first few weeks of college can be draining, so as I mentioned earlier in this manual:

BE GENTLE WITH YOURSELF. BE PATIENT WITH YOURSELF

- For the parents, I know you miss your baby but encourage them to fight through their fear and panic. Both of you will appreciate it after it's all said and done.
- Find other parents with first-time college students and form support networks to share information and advice on how to navigate the process.

- Plan time, specific times to travel home for the weekends and holidays if possible. If you're an out of state student or international student, this could get a little expensive but proper planning can help you navigate times that you want to travel home.

- If you attend college in a location where you have extended family, reach out to them so that they know you're close by and can provide assistance. I loved having family in surrounding cities because they could access me in the event my mother was unable to. They were able to provide home cooked meals and comfort while away.

- Last but not least, if you're feeling overwhelmed, anxious, depressed, consistently sad, or not motivated, talk with your schools counselor, your RA, mentor, someone connected to the same faith as you, your parents, friends, or someone you connect with that will listen and offer the support you need. Please do not feel that you have to suffer in silence or suffer at all. If the best decision is to take a break from school, there is no judgment and you must do what's in the best interest for you.

If you're like most incoming freshmen, you probably have early morning classes because it's a required course and they only offer it between 8:30 and 9:15 AM. If you're not a morning person, this is probably going to be a little challenging for you but I advise to either wait to take that course when it's offered at a later time or have multiple alarm clocks that will assist you with getting up because professors will count you as absent if you're not in class by a set time. There's usually a grace period that's offered but it's up to you to learn what that grace period is. Of course, if you have any type of disability needs, this should be established up front in order to give you the support that you need to navigate classes. Absent this, only true emergencies can be utilized for missing a class. This is important to stress because enrolling in a class and failing is very expensive in college. I learned this lesson the hard way. I enrolled in a required course at 8:00 AM for Mondays, Wednesdays, and Fridays. As a morning person, this wasn't a bad setup for me, however, once I realized the class was on the other side of campus, I started putting it off. I figured that since it was an easy class and with good grades, I could still get by. That wasn't the case and I ended up failing the class due to attendance. Here is the tricky and expensive equation:

8:00 AM Class x 3 credit hours = $600; Failed 8:00 AM Class x 3 credit hours=$600
Total: $1200

If this little botched math equation confuses you, then let me break it down. Your scholarship/loan/grant etc. pays for each class you enroll in. If you pass the course, great. Your money was well invested and used. If you fail the class for any reason, you have to make the course up and pay the amount again; so you pretty much throw money away when you fail a course vs. dropping a course. All colleges have protocol in place if a student needs or wants to drop a class before charging them for it. Make sure you understand the magnitude of how this can affect you financially when making a decision about your classes.

As a newcomer, most of your classes will be required courses that must be taken prior to taking electives and classes in your major. These are your courses similar to classes from high school like math, history, language, etc. FYI, you will be required to take a foreign language at most universities; so get a head start by choosing a language in high school that you can breeze through in college. I did it completely backwards and made it hard for myself. I took French in high school because I wanted to eat French food but ended up taking Spanish in college. Go figure. I struggled tremendously! I don't know what possessed me to do that but thankfully, I was fortunate enough to have instructors that were patient and, most of all, lenient with me so that I was able to pass Spanish I and II. Another thing to keep in mind is that your university may require you to perform a certain amount of community service hours that can be completed in most settings that are in the education or non-profit sector.

One of the most exciting things that really united students was eating at the cafeteria or café, as it's mostly referred to. This was the time to hang out with friends over some pretty decent food. I loved the days our café would host specialty food days and have live music. This was where my hall mates and I would spend hours over food and laughs about boys, clothes, classes, home, and anything worthy of laughing about. It was in the café that we huddled together, fought through the crowd and fought through our insecurities of looking weird while getting food. This is a great place to break the sadness of missing home. If you hang in there for a little bit longer, before you realize it, your new circle of friends will be added to your extended family and the days won't feel as lonely. Here are a few other pointers to consider as a freshman to help ease your way into college:

- Going out really pays off. Even if you are an introvert, go bowling or visit your local museum; you get to hang out with friends and get the college experience.
- Do not just sit in your room, whether it is in a dorm or your house, during the weekend. Go for a run or a walk. Get to know your campus; explore academic buildings you don't usually go to.
- Make friends with the students who are sitting next to you in class. They will make your classroom experience so much better and you can borrow class notes from them if you get sick.
- Say hello to your professors! Chances are you will have them again later on, in your college career. Even if you are in a class with over 100

students, if they already know who you are and know you by name, meeting them during office hours will be so much easier.

- Bring enough clothing with you to school that you can go two weeks between washings. This will save you money in the long run.
- Don't put your alarm clock anywhere you can reach it. Make yourself get out of bed to turn it off if you're in need of an even more strict solution
- Find out what resources your school offers. Many universities have free tech support centers, health centers, seminars, and more.
- Be confident, get out of your comfort zone and try new things.

CHAPTER 5

Selecting A Major. How?!

You've done the work to get through your first semester of college and you're feeling comfortable with campus life. You made it through and are finally able to begin to take electives and courses in your field of study or courses of what you desire to major in. This can be tricky because there are so many things that you want to do and you really want to find a way to narrow it down. This is probably going to be one of the most important sections in this book because majoring in a wrong field can leave you unemployed and having to go back to take additional courses so that your degree will be relevant. This is not the decision that you'd want to play "follow your peers" on. Just because it looks popular and fun doesn't mean it's the major for you. This is the time that you REALLY need to speak with your Academic Advisor to discuss the things you would like to do and the best major to study to help you accomplish your goal. What you'll discover is that you can major in almost anything at college. Some majors are more recognized than others. Some majors or degrees will just be decorations for your parent's wall mantel and that's it.

You'll want to select a major that will add value to the working class world and aligns with your skillset. This is the time that you really need to tap into those things that you're really good at and what you generally do very well. In order to assist in this area, explore the opportunities to volunteer or intern in your field of interest. Some people automatically know what they want to be when they grow up and for others, it's not really clear. Sometimes, students select majors based on how easy and how popular it is. I have literally met individuals with degrees in Fine Arts, Literature, or a foreign language and wasn't able to use it in the work sector. In case you weren't aware, you can major in a field of study and also minor in another field of interest that helps connect the two when you begin applying for jobs. That's the ultimate goal of attending college so that you can implement those things from education into the work world, to make the world and processes a better place. There are some majors that will increase your chances of getting into certain professional fields. For example, if you want to be a medical doctor, you will need to major in a field that will benefit you when you actually apply to medical school. You should focus on majors such as Biology, Science, Nursing, etc. vs. majors such as Psychology, Political Science, Sports, etc. These are majors that are going to best prepare you for studying medicine. Another example is if you decide you want to be an attorney.

In this case, you should major in fields that hone your reading and writing skills. Majors such as Communication, Political Science, and Public Administration are ideal to prepare you for law school. If you want to become a teacher, you should major in Education, in addition to completing the necessary internship programs. There will also be prerequisite courses meaning, courses that are required before you can select a major. Here are a few examples of majors and minors that can offer some insight into how you can navigate this process and select a major that pays for itself once you graduate:

- Business Administration (this degree is great if you pair it with minors such as accounting, finance, human resource, marketing).

- Communication (this degree is ideal if you pair it with minors such as mass media, journalism, public relations).

- Education (early childhood education, special education, high school education).

- Engineer (mechanical and aerospace, chemical, electrical and computer).

- Information Technology (database management, software development).

This, by no means, is a recommendation or suggestion of what to major or minor in. This only serves as examples on how you, the student, can pair a major and minor, and establishes a great foundation to getting employed upon graduation. The main goal of attending college is to increase your knowledge and then, to give that knowledge back to the world in some form of employment. I hadn't met too many people along the way that completed college just for fun or just for the hell of it. Those groups generally fell off after about the 2nd year of college.

If you decide to major in studies such as music, art, psychology, sports, math, etc., it will be vitally important to identify what your goal is with these majors and to do your research on how you will incorporate them into the work sector. I'll speak more about entrepreneurship because I know some college grads are very ambitious and able to start their business right after graduating. I believe that it's wise to have a plan for whichever direction you plan to take. When I was attending college, we used to see this chart that outlined the salary of individuals with college degrees vs. individuals without degrees. That was an encouraging chart, however, I wish there would have been information to show the salaries among different majors because it would have made a lot of students choose differently. If I could do it all over again, I would have majored in Business Administration, along with a minor in Public

Relations, because I enjoy working in the business, public, and entrepreneur sector. While I used my Criminal Justice degree very well, I would have added more value to it that could have gotten my feet in other industries easier. I know students who majored in degrees such as Math because they wanted to teach math in a school setting, however, they didn't take any courses in Education which could have given them more options if they decided they didn't want to teach any longer.

Due to the increasing cost of tuition, you certainly want to ensure you select a major that will be helpful in paying towards your student loans. As a disclaimer, there is nothing that can truly predict your success when it comes to your decision of what to major in, however, there are things that you can do that will increase your chances of success.

Important major considerations include:

- Overall program cost.
- Salary expectations.
- Employment rates for employees in the field.
- Advanced degree opportunities.

Ultimately, you must decide which field will offer the best return-on-investment, or ROI, for your postsecondary education. According to a recent report from the University of La Verne, roughly half of all college freshmen enter college undecided about their major. Additionally, as many as 70% will change their major at least once during the course of their four-year degree program; the majority of these students change their major at least three times. Many students worry that changing their major will delay graduation and, as a result, significantly increase their overall tuition costs. However, a study at Western Kentucky University found that shifting major fields had a minimal impact on planned graduation times. Furthermore, the data showed that full-time students, who changed majors at least once, reported higher graduation rates than those who remained in the same field for their entire bachelor's program. With this in mind, remember these points:

- It's ok if you select a major and decide to go in a different direction. It's better to change it now than wait until it's time to graduate.

- It's okay to follow the money. You have more than enough time to pursue passions. Matter of fact, you can do both but chase the money while you're young and have the capacity to take on more academic and work responsibilities. As you get older, you'll be ready to coast instead of doing so much.

- Ask for feedback or talk to someone who is actually working in a field that you would want to work in. You ever heard the saying, "I want to be like you when I grow up?" Think like that and find people who you want to be like when you grow up. Declaring a major isn't a decision you have to make alone. Leaning on others can help you realize things you wouldn't have come to know on your own. Ask your friends and family what they think your strong traits are.

- Follow your dreams, no matter how large or small they may be. This is your life and you have to live it to your desire. You really can be whatever you desire to be. Just be ready to put in the necessary work to make it happen. Develop your plan of action and take action!

CHAPTER 6

Managing Your Independence As A College Student. How?!

If you're like college students who were the first ones in your family to attend college, this is probably your first real taste of independence. You've now embarked upon a territory in which you can pretty much play by your own rules. You don't have the headache of parents giving you a curfew or telling you what's appropriate or inappropriate to wear. You can go and come as you please and you can do as much of anything you want without much adult supervision. While this sounds fun and is fun, this is the time that you have to exercise the most discipline than you've ever had because temptation and peer pressure is constantly knocking at your door. Your fist year of college can literally be lost to partying and overindulging in everything that's unhealthy or not good for you in general, from food to sex. Don't get me wrong, I won't be the bearer of bad news and preach to you about all of the things not to do because you probably already know. Your parents have already had the conversations with you. If you don't know and no one has informed you, then you will learn from trial and error. I promise. What I will suggest is to be responsible about everything you do. Peer pressure is real; it's easy to fall prey to what everyone else is doing and the need to fit in.

Drug use and suicide rates on college campuses have increased over the years and it seems to keep inclining instead of declining. Did college cause these matters? Who's to say but I can understand how. I remember when I was in college and learned the harrowing story about a college student that walked into their dorm room and found their suite mate hanging by way of committing suicide. Of course this was extremely traumatizing for the student who discovered it and even more painful for the victim's family. I don't know if there was a suicide note left or not, but these feelings are very real and it's important to know that there are boundless amounts of support and information that you can access if you're feeling like you're falling into thoughts and behaviors of suicide or self-harm.

Drug use is always one of the most highly discussed topics on college campuses and rightfully so because it's readily available, with the most accessible being alcohol. "YES", alcohol is a drug and "YES", it has been one of the most deadly drugs on college campuses. The issue with alcohol is that you can get access to it easily on college, even being underage. My first experience with getting drunk was my freshman year and it was the last time I would ever drink that much. Getting ready for a party on "college club night", I decided to "turn" up with my friends by drinking cups of tequila because I wanted to have major fun. That was a horrible idea! Not only did I miss the party, but I caused my other friends who were "babysitting" me to miss the party as well. I got sick and had a major hangover the following day, and not to forget the embarrassment of the whole thing after hearing my friends laugh about how I was acting. Some of the night was a fleeting memory and other parts of the night came back vividly. My experience was one of the more fortunate ones in comparison to other stories of excessive drinking that turned fatal. Thankfully, I was able to learn from that experience and started exercising responsibility by only drinking at the appropriate and legal age of 21 and also, only having one drink with friends and never going over the limit. Alcohol was the only drug that I engaged in but there were other students that I knew who were into marijuana. That seemed so scary to me because they always looked out of their minds or as they were called "stoned".

Upon my graduation from college, I decided that I wanted to be a counselor and went into the field of behavioral health and substance abuse treatment. It was at this time that I counseled and treated a lot of college students for drug abuse cases. It was at this time that I read about how students were dying as a result of drug overdoses, car accidents, or other accidents as a result of drug use. What does this mean for you? Here's a little list of support items that can carry you a long way in college as an independent adult:

- If you're not interested in drugs...don't try them and don't listen to your peers that try to convince you to try them.

- If you're curious about trying a drug but afraid...seek guidance from your counselors or someone that you're close with that can give you an unbiased ear to hear what you're dealing with. Identify the reasons you're curios about experimenting with drugs. Are you interested because you think it will make you look cool or become part of the popular crowd? Are you interested because you feel stressed out or anxious and want something to "level" you out? Whatever the reason may be, find out "why".

- Don't underestimate how a little alcohol can affect you. This is very important for young women. Our bodies digest alcohol at a slower rate than guys, so it's easier for us to have a higher Blood Alcohol Count (BAC) than guys with fewer drinks. Why does this matter? It matters because if you were to be approached by a law enforcement officer or campus police and you appear to be under the influence, they can legally issue you a breathalyzer test that will determine if you're over or under the legal drinking level/limit, which in most states is 0.08.

- Never accept any type of drug from someone you don't know. Even if you do know them, be very cautious about accepting drinks or drugs during parties or other events where there are lots of people around. This increases the potential of drugs and alcohol being laced with other foreign and synthetic substances that can be fatal.

- Never drink the "punch". The punch is very misleading. With all of the fruit, it appears completely innocent. Believe me. It's not and it generally contains more alcohol than the average amount in beer and liquor combined.

- Never drive or ride with friends that are under the influence. Even if they try to convince you that they're "fine". Even if you feel like "superman" or "superwoman", you should never get behind the wheel of a vehicle if you've had any substance that has impaired your abilities. This could lead to a lifetime of trouble that will follow and haunt you for a long time. Let's not even talk about how it could end fatally.

Let's talk about suicide. Life can, and will, be hard at times and being in college comes with a lot of pressures. Because you're independent, you're working to establish your identity. Who you are and what makes you "you". College has a lot of "outlets" for individuals that are looking to discover who they are. For some, it's the need to belong and to fit in. Some people achieve this through joining sororities or fraternities. Some students do it through playing sports or joining the college band. Don't get me wrong. These aren't the only reasons but for a lot of students, it's for an identity. It always amazed me to see the guy that was labeled a nerd in high school but, once enrolled in college and gravitating toward certain crowds, the once nerd is now the hot stud on campus! I wish I could tell you how many people I met upon first starting college and we were all scared, goofy, and inexperienced little 17 and 18 year olds trying to discover ourselves. It came out in the way we dressed. For some, it came in the form of changing their religious beliefs, and for others, it was through whatever methods that would make them most popular.

I lived in the freshman dorm on the 7th floor. It was a long double-room hallway with two girls to each room. The total number of girls was around 60 and out of the 60, close to one-third became exotic dancers or "strippers" as they were called. I can't say that it wasn't tempting because they received a lot of attention; good and bad, and they were earning money. Who wouldn't want to be known as being sexy with all the men/women flocking to you? Well, not to get too far off track, college is the place that you can become lost and consumed in and if you're not careful, it can leave you feeling vulnerable and intimidated. Because of these feelings and not having an outlet for some, the next thing to try was engaging in nonproductive behavior such as drug use and even contemplating suicide. Read the line below very carefully:

"You are important. You are loved. You are valued. You can make it. It may hurt right now but if you hang in there, you can get the support you need and you can/will survive." "It may seem difficult and confusing but you can get through it." "There is nothing that you have done that is unforgivable or too bad that you cannot recover."

Research conducted through the Suicide Prevention Resource Center states that suicide is the leading cause of death among college and university students in the United States. 1,000 students on college campuses take their life each year and over half have suicidal thoughts and have attempted suicide. Parents, friends, and loved ones can oftentimes miss signs because at college, it's so easy to fly under the radar. It's so easy to miss potential warning signs and it's challenging to spot the covert signs that the college student doesn't show or mention because they are afraid of the attention that would come with acknowledging their internal struggles and feeling guilty about acknowledging their inadequacies of coping with life. This is the normal stuff that everyone faces in life but in college, it can feel embarrassing, unpopular, or weak. There are a lot of pressures in college that we forget about as adults and assume that nothing more than class and partying could be going on with our students. Well, let me tell you. From someone who has been on both sides of the coin as a former college student and now as an adult/counselor/coach, there are stressors that are really relevant and sensitive to college students that may not be relevant to others. For example, if you don't have the finances to supply yourself with a nice wardrobe or the latest fashion, this can be devastating. Of course to the adult, this is a no-brainer right? How dare we get caught up in the material things? But for the college student, this says, "I don't have the means to fit in with the "in" crowd." We notice that the students with the "hypest" and "dopest" gear got most of the attention.

Now let's deviate to briefly acknowledge the dating game and relationships. Through observation, most of the college girls were attracted to the guys who had money, the latest fashion, and the car to drive girls around in because they exuded the confidence that many students wanted. This sometimes...oftentimes, led to relationship woes. The advice I would give to any college student, male or female, when it comes to dating is:

- If you have a high school sweetheart and the two of you have separate plans after you graduate from high school, it's best to have a discussion of where the two of you want to be long-term. College and dating can add a lot of pressure to both parties and if things don't work out, it can leave you both feeling devastated. It's totally okay if the two of you

decide to take a break or hook back up when you finish college.
- Focus as much as possible on establishing friendships before entering into relationships. This goes for platonic and romantic ones.
- Date responsibly.
- Avoid toxic and abusive people. This is for guys and girls.

One year as a freshman, a friend and I were walking to the student union. This was the hub for students when we weren't in class or at the café. This was where students hung out on the "yard" which felt more like a fashion runway or the walk of shame, depending on what category you fell in. On this particular day, it was pretty sparse with students as mostly everyone was either in class or chilling in their dorm room. We decided to go down to check our mail and there were two guys from the football team that both my friend and I knew. One of the guys we knew and liked more than the other because we just did. As we were walking inside, the guy that we really didn't like decided to attempt to bully me by calling me a "BITCH". Of course, being the individual I was, I wasn't going to allow someone to disrespect me in that manner; I commenced to curse him out and drag him for the disrespectful and immature boy he was, but on the inside, I was truly shaken because I had never had that experience. The argument was brutal with us literally shouting at each other and me being pulled away back to my dorm room. I immediately got on the phone to call every male friend I had that I knew would bring him much harm and pain because he disrespected me. After being talked down off of that ledge, I decided to drop it because I felt I handled myself fairly well and it was water under the bridge. Apparently, he didn't feel the same way and continued the saga by pitting his girlfriend and her friends against me. Days that I would walk to the café by myself, they would all stand on the side of the building tossing insults and making threats to harm me. They even went as far as attempting to get one of the female basketball players in on the action. On the inside, I was sort of scared but I also had to maintain my strength. I couldn't allow my friends to see me shaken, so I kept my cool. I walked with my head held high and I didn't entertain their insults but inside my dorm room, I called home and spoke to my mom about transferring to another school. This incident was stressful for me because it was attempting to rob me of my peace and comfort that I had on campus and it made me dread facing the next day. I wasn't a fighter but I could if I needed to. With brothers and boy cousins that teased you when you were little, you learned to take up for yourself. Absent this, I no longer wanted to go to my school. Of course my mother talked me out of it because I never told her what the real problem was and the nonsense eventually subsided. School let out for summer break and when I returned, the same guy became so infatuated with me that he didn't "recall" the issue we had the previous semester. How was I able to navigate this situation without it completely destroying my college experience? I had enough of what is termed "protective" factors that allowed me to cope differently than other students who may have been exposed to more risk factors than protective ones. Why is this relevant? It's relevant because these factors have been strong predictors of suicidal thoughts, ideas, and plans. Because these thoughts and ideas can increase in college, it's so important to discuss that in this book, to offer insight and support to parents, teachers, students, or whoever else may flip through the pages. What are protective and risk factors? Well, here goes:

Protective Factors: Protective factors determine how well you respond to conflict and challenges. Protective factors listed below, give the individual the capacity to cope positively in the face of adversities and discomfort. This is called resilience. Having strong protective factors helps to safeguard you from engaging in certain behaviors such as illicit drug use, violence, and suicidal thoughts and plans that could be detrimental to your growth and development as a youth and into adulthood. Some examples of

Protective Factors are:

- Psychological or emotional well-being, positive mood
- Positive beliefs about yourself and hopes and plans for your future
- Problem-solving and coping skills, including conflict resolution
- Frustration tolerance and ability to regulate emotions
- Healthy self-esteem
- Spiritual beliefs or regular religious practice or attendance
- Cultural and religious beliefs that affirm life and discourage suicide
- A sense of responsibility to family or friends, not wanting to hurt family or friends
- Physical activity, especially aerobic activity

Social Support Protective Factors

- Family: Support from, and connectedness to family; closeness to, or strong relationship with parents, parental involvement
- Friends: Social involvement and support from friendships and romantic relationships
- Teachers, mentors, and other adults, such as student group leaders, coaches, faith leaders, and workplace supervisors: Concern, understanding, and caring
- Ongoing support and support to call on in times of crises

School and Community Factors

- Supportive and inclusive peer and mentor environment
- A sense of connectedness to school and/or belonging within the school community
- Availability and accessibility of student support services and personnel

- Involvement in extracurricular activities, e.g., joining a student club or organization
- Access to effective care for mental, physical, and substance abuse disorders
- Restricted access to lethal means, especially firearms (e.g., firearms are not allowed on campus)
- Monitoring and control of alcohol use

Risk Factors: Risk factors are those attributes that decrease ones resilience and make it more challenging to cope with life. Risk factors refer to characteristics that are associated with suicide. People who are affected by one or more risk factors may have a greater probability of suicidal behavior. This does not mean that the individual will commit suicide. This is only to discuss behaviors. Some risk factors cannot be changed—such as a previous suicide attempt—but they can be used to help identify someone who may be vulnerable to suicide.

Behavioral Health Issues & Disorders:

- Depressive disorders
- Substance abuse or dependence (alcohol and other drugs)
- Delinquency/Conduct disorders
- Other disorders (e.g., anxiety disorders, eating disorders)
- Previous suicide attempts
- Self-injury (without intent to die)

Individual Characteristics:

- Hopelessness
- Loneliness
- Social alienation and isolation, lack of belonging
- Anger, hostility
- Risky behavior, impulsivity
- Low stress and frustration tolerance
- Poor problem-solving or coping skills
- Perception of being a burden (e.g., to family and friends)

Adverse/Stressful Life Circumstances:

- Interpersonal difficulties or losses (e.g., relationship breakup, dating violence)
- School or work problems
- Financial problems
- Physical, sexual, and/or psychological abuse (current and/or previous)
- Chronic physical illness or disability
- Insomnia and nightmares

Family Characteristics:

- Family history of suicide or suicidal behavior
- Parental mental health problems
- Family violence or abuse (current and/or previous)
- Family instability and/or loss
- Lack of parental support

School & Community Factors:

- Limited access to effective care for health, mental health, or substance abuse disorders
- Stigma associated with seeking care
- Negative social and emotional environment, including negative attitudes, beliefs, feelings, and interactions of staff and students
- Exposure to stigma and discrimination against students based on sexual orientation, gender identity, race and ethnicity, disability, or physical characteristics (such as being overweight)
- Access to lethal means
- Exposure to media normalizing or glamorizing suicide

I want to be 100% clear that this is not an exhaustive or exclusive list of factors that can predict or dictate how or if a student will act on suicidal thoughts, however, this is a list that can serve as a guide to students and parents to ensure you are equipped with the knowledge on the areas you can grow and improve as a student and as a parent. At the end of the day, there are no absolutes or guarantees, and just because one may have more protective factors doesn't mean that they can't fall prey to dangerous behavior.

If you or a friend are scared, worried, fearful, afraid, depressed, sad, overly happy, overly sad, lack motivation, having suicidal thoughts and ideas, self-harming, or attempting to commit suicide, please call this number to get the help and support you need and deserve:

1-800-273-8255

Let's Talk About Sex!

I know I know. This section will probably make parents uncomfortable but there's no need in avoiding this topic because it's BIG BIG on college campuses and it happens. This section will actually be more tolerable than you'd imagine, so here it goes. To the college student who now has unlimited freedom without adult supervision, this is the time to put all of the knowledge you learned in Sex Ed in high school to use. I'll make it real simple in this section:

- Abstinence is the best method to prevent contracting an STD or having an unplanned/unwanted pregnancy. Research states that nationally, unplanned births account for nearly one in 10 dropouts among female students at community colleges, and 7 percent of dropouts among community college students overall.4 The impact on students is significant—61 percent of community college students who have children after enrolling do not finish their education, which is 65 percent higher than women who do not have children while in college. As far as the prevalence of STD rates and transmission rates, a recent report from the Centers For Disease Control and Prevention revealed that certain curable sexually transmitted infections, namely syphilis, chlamydia, and gonorrhea, are on the rise among young adults ages 15 to 24. Young women in particular are contracting syphilis at alarming rates; the rate of infection increasing by 36% from 2015 to 2016. If left untreated, syphilis can cause blindness, infertility, and strokes. Additionally, a recent study shows that 1 in 9 American men, ages 18 to 69, has the human papilloma virus, better known as HPV. In some cases, HPV can cause genital warts or even cancer. And the CDC anticipates the problem only getting worse.

- If you are going to be sexually active, ALWAYS use protection. The condom, when used correctly, is still the most effective way in preventing unwanted pregnancies and preventing the spread or contraction of most STD's or STI's. Mostly because there are some STI's that condom use does not provide protection against and that's HSV 2.

- Use condoms even if you're using another form of birth control. While condoms and birth control are effective in preventing pregnancies, neither are 100% effective, meaning that there's still a small possibility of one becoming pregnant.

- Remember, oral sex is still a form of sex and STD's can be transmitted through this route. There are dental dams that are specific to protecting against oral STD's.

- Try to be consistent with one partner and determine if that one person is able to be consistent with you. Having multiple sexual partners increases the chances of contracting an STD.

- Utilize your on-campus health center or ensure that you have a primary care doctor to perform regular STD test. If you ever have a situation in which a condom was not utilized or the condom broke, go to your on-campus health center so that testing can be performed immediately and also discussions on how to prevent a pregnancy from taking place. Timing is of the essence in all of these cases and it's generally a small window; 12-48 hours in order to reverse some things that could occur such as transmission of HIV virus and pregnancy.

Remember, you are responsible for your choices and decisions and I advise you to choose wisely. Be very selective about who you entertain and never judge a book by it's cover; meaning in cases like making a decision to be sexually involved with an individual, it should never be based on their looks to determine their STD status. A person's looks, status, or material accumulation is not a defense against STD's. You cannot look at a person and "tell" that they don't or do have an STD. Always use protection. Regardless of how much you may love each other or how they may have sworn to exclusiveness with you and only you. It's better to be safe now than sorry later.

BEWARE of Your Surroundings

Keeping pace with your new level of independence, it's important to include this message in this book.

ALWAYS INCORPORATE A BUDDY SYSTEM!!!!
A "buddy" system is a concept of having a system in which you are never alone on campus or away from campus outside of going to class or going to a job offsite. The buddy system is to be enacted during after hours when there is not a huge presence of students or faculty in which you and your friends can

be visible in the event something were to happen, and definitely during off-campus activities. Unfortunately, sexual assaults on college campuses are real and they have scarred a lot of people and some have even been fatal. Although research is continuing to advance in the area of sexual assaults on campus, this is a serious matter that has impacted college students in a very harsh and real way. Having a buddy system in which you have one or more persons with you when you leave campus for nightlife events decreases the chances of being sexually assaulted. To better explain, here are a few pointers/tips to incorporate:

- Partner with one or more friends during after hours campus activities.

- If you're going out on a date, be sure to get the person's license plate information, car description, and ask for ID to ensure the person is who they say they are.

- Do not leave a venue with anyone that you do

not feel comfortable with or that you just met unless you're prepared to entertain what comes with it.

- Never accept drinks from a stranger or a drink that you did not see being made by a bartender. If you've never heard of the term called "DATE RAPE", Google it now!

- Even when on campus, if it's after hours, be sure to have a buddy to accompany you or ask campus police for escort services.

- Do not text and walk at night.

- Do not text in your parked car at night. Why is this relevant? Because this is an open invitation for a lurker to attack while you're unassuming and unaware.

- If you go out with a buddy or group, leave with that buddy or group. Never allow your friend to talk you into "leaving" them alone.

- Make the pact before leaving out that

everyone that comes together will leave together.

- Do not allow your friends to get drunk or be under the influence of drugs and leave them alone with strangers. Keep an eye on them and get them to a safe location ASAP.

New found independence is a great thing but it comes with loads of responsibility. You can have a great time in college but it can all change if you're unaware of things that can sidetrack you and cause problems.

CHAPTER 7

Pledging. What's The Big Deal about Greek Life?!

I'm not apart of any sorority, but I have countless of friends and families that are, and who were, willing to share some helpful insight into Greek life. Sorority and fraternity life is major on college campuses and 1st "Geners" are mostly familiar with sororities and frats by knowing or seeing someone with these cool and different shaped letters and colors on their shirts, or watching a step show or seeing hand symbols thrown up at a party. Absent those things, it's not a lot that you know until you get on campus and begin to see the parties they throw and see everyone hanging out together wearing the same colors and making their signature Greek call that you become mesmerized. You want to know what's the big deal and at some point, may be led to inquire about how to become a part of it all.

At one point of my collegiate experience, I briefly explored pledging but learned really quickly that it wasn't for me. I had my own personal philosophies regarding Greek life and the authenticity of the individuals that were members. Now, I'm able to see some of the value of being connected but at the end of the day, it wasn't the path for me. That may not be the case for you but I want to give you some pointers that I learned and also lessons from some of my Greek friends. To begin, I would recommend that you learn as much as you can about the Greek organization you're interested in. It's so important to have knowledge about whom you're pledging your allegiance to and which Greek letters you will be representing. While there are many organizations to connect with and lots of pressure to go with a certain sorority or frat, you should do your own research and homework before making a decision. There are a lot of people that pledged a certain Greek organization because their friend or family member is a part of that group. This is cool too. Whatever helps make the connection for you and if that's what you decide to do, then by all means. Personally, I feel it's necessary to be as knowledgeable as possible because that will help you get your foot in the door. You may, or may not, know but while Greek life looks fun and exciting, they do have standards that students and pledges have to meet in order to begin the process. These are a few of the things I learned from Greek friends and my own personal experience:

- Your grades must be on point. Most Greek organizations require at least a 3.0 at the time of expressing formal interest.

- How do you find out about joining? When I was in undergraduate studies, I remember hearing discussions about a "rush" meeting for Delta Sigma Theta and I became curios because the girls I knew that was interested were super excited. They were reviewing their grades on the phone with their sister or mother that was a Delta or talking with other students that were already Delta's.

- It's really important to attend the Rush in order to make your interest known. Rush is also a platform for Greek leaders to peruse the room to determine who would be a good fit to join their organization.

- You will receive information about the organization.

- Each sorority and fraternity probably has their own unique process, but this offers some foundational understanding.

- You'll probably see others that are interested in joining that you don't like and that probably don't like you at the time.

- Hazing is illegal but it happens. From research, some colleges have completely banned Greek life on campus.

- It's extremely competitive and you may not get selected the first time. If this is the case, don't give up if that's your goal.

- Being involved and connected is a plus. Partnering with community service activities that the organization sponsors is a plus.

- You will more than likely need references from someone that's already a member of the organization.

- It will cost money. You will likely find out about the fees once you attend the Rush meeting or once you receive your acceptance letter.

- You will have to ensure you maintain good academic standing. This is a great benefit to Greek life.

- If you get accepted, congratulations! If you don't get accepted, don't get discouraged. If you really want it, keep going after it. If you don't want to move forward, then it's no harm no foul.

Getting accepted into a Greek organization is big deal for a lot of students and it becomes an act of honor once starting the process. I could always tell when someone was "underground" as we used to call it because pledges became completely invisible. They would be extremely discreet in their day-to day life on campus and then, they would disappear for a few days. I know because my college roommate was on line and I rarely saw her once she started the process. There were a lot of things I observed and learned that I won't share because you'll see and learn soon enough if you or someone you're close to decides to pledge. I remember my best friend pledged at her college in Virginia. I attended her probate and remembered thinking how much smaller she had gotten. She was so tiny and I knew it was because she was on the grind with pledging and that she had been through a rigorous process. Probates were an exciting and emotional time for all involved because it was the coming out and finalization of the process of the sisterhood or brotherhood. I enjoyed each event because it was an invitation to party and celebrate. This is where you'll see the pledges "cross" and they'll display their line names and numbers. This part was always funny for the frats because the guys would be clean-shaven and look like adult newborn babies. For the ladies, it was mostly weight loss. Talk about a reason to join right? At the end of the day, it's all about what you make of it. You will become popular on campus if you weren't before. People will want to be connected to you just because you are part of sorority or fraternity. You and other pledges will probably become the best of friends and soon be incorporated into each other's circle. Thankfully, my college roommate and I remained really good friends and nothing much shifted in our circle of four. To learn more about Greek life on your campus, get involved and ask questions of the people you see that represents a particular organization. Also, most campuses have a division in Student Affairs and that's an ideal place to begin the search too!

CHAPTER 8

What's Really Real About The "Real World"?

While you're enrolled in college, this is the best time to maximize opportunities to get employed upon graduation. Your newness to the workforce and lack of experience is golden to employers that want to hire individuals who can be easily trained and offered minimum pay in order to meet their demands. As a former Hiring Manager, this is the best advice related to getting prepared for the work world that I can offer. It's important to capitalize off of your youth and innocence now while people are likely to be more understanding of mistakes you'll make along the way verses when you're older and have more experience and wisdom. When I was an undergraduate, I highly underestimated Career Services which is a department on most campuses that is designed to offer students support and assistance in developing their resumes, identifying internship, co-op, and work study opportunities. This was the office that I neglected the most but wished I could turn back the hands of time in order to capitalize on the benefits. Friends of mine who had utilized their services had a leg up on those of us who didn't. For instance, this department was incremental in getting students in the door to federal government. This was a huge plus because at that time, federal government employment offered a decent salary, longevity to individuals that wanted to build a steady career, and also offered positions with great chances for promotion. To be honest, I didn't hear about Career Services too much until after I had graduated. Nonetheless, this department should be in a student's top 5 departments to connect with.

You'll be glad you did once you realize that although your youthfulness may have an advantage, it's still a common practice for employers to say, "You don't have enough experience." Then you become caught in the cycle of frustration in which you scream "HOW CAN I GET THE EXPERIENCE IF NO PLACE IS WILLING TO HIRE ME???!!!" To avoid this as much as possible, these are some of the things you, as the college student, can consider:

- Go to Career Service and register. Sign up for resume writing assistance and any other services offered.

- Identify internships and work-study programs. It may not necessarily be in your major but it may offer you the chance to gain work experience and income.

- Apply for internships and work-study programs early. Remember that the early bird catches the worm. This is a very true saying.

- Research opportunities outside of campus. The Internet is ideal. With a simple Google search on internships, a wealth of information will come up.

- Be a GO-GETTER!!!! The world is your oyster. This is the time to maximize your youthfulness and vigor. Do not be afraid to take chances. Speak to strangers. Ask questions. Get involved. Lend a helping hand even if it doesn't benefit you. Be kind, especially with adults. You never know who's paying attention and can end up being a blessing to your life. This type of energy will land you in so many great opportunities. I promise!

- Show respect. ALWAYS. I'm from the South where we were taught to say "thank you", "yes ma'am", "no ma'am", "yes sir", and "no sir". While this may sound dated and out of style, it still gets me in the door to this very day. This not only gets you ahead in your career path, but it will get you ahead in life. People love to be respected. I offer this courtesy to everyone. You never know that the very person you give respect to could be the person that holds the power to your next internship, job, or work-study. Me personally, I don't make any discretion based off of how someone "looks" to determine if I will respect them or not. You get back what you put out.

- Research your "dream" career. Learn as much about the profession as you possibly can. There are several benefits rooted in this with one being, you are able to be articulate about what you want to do when you speak with people about your dream. This also tells the Universe that you are aligning yourself for this opportunity to manifest in your life.

- Remember that all jobs matter. Any form of employment that you get the chance to connect with is a plus. You will learn various skills that can help you be a better professional in your dream job.

- Look for employment and internship opportunities BEFORE your summer break. If you're unable to identify internship opportunities, begin applying for jobs that will allow you to start once you've completed the semester. If you're already employed, then that's awesome. You're ahead of the game. During my summer breaks, I applied to local jobs through an employment agency. I worked in industrial roles, administrative, internships, and co-ops. I gained a wealth of skill sets that I was able to apply in my profession.

- Remain confident in the process and most of all, remain consistent. Although getting your professional life on track while in college can be challenging, it's worth every moment you invest in it.

CHAPTER 9

You Did It! (Graduation) Now What?

The time and day has come where you are FINALLY moving on and preparing for graduation! This is one of the most surreal feelings of accomplishment that you will feel. Not the only one but definitely one of many. This is the time where things are winding down and you're taking the final steps towards completing your college requirements in order to receive your cap/gown and your graduation date. This is the time in which you will need to ensure that you have met ALL of your college requirements because this can sneak up on you and ruin your entire day if you haven't. It will be vitally important that you go to the Bursar's Office to ensure that there are not any outstanding balances on your student account. You will need to have your transcripts pulled to ensure that you've met all of the academic requirements for your major. You will need to make sure you've completed any required community service projects for the University and you'll want to make sure that you don't have any failed classes that you didn't make up. I saw so many students miss their graduation as a result of some of these mistakes. This does not have to be you when you handle your business in advance. These are some reminders for preparing for graduation:

- Be proactive. Do not wait until the last minute to check these things out.

- Ask for assistance if there is something you don't understand.

- Don't be afraid to face the music. If you slacked off and you have to stay behind an extra semester, then so be it. Finish it up and get your degree. You've come too far to give up now!

- Get that difficult class out of the way (math, foreign language, etc.)

- Monitor your GPA. Don't settle for C's. Although a C is considered passing, it bottoms your GPA out and can leave you with a 2.0 easily. Why is this important? You'll know once you see your peers with all of their beautiful and colorful chords they get with their cap and gown as a demonstration of academic achievement and success. You will feel that pressure and it will be very real. Not just for the pressure from your peers, which is a good thing, but strive for this achievement for yourself. It's an accomplishment that you will be grateful for.

You have to be proactive in knowing what's going on with your college plan. Graduation planning can be overwhelming especially if you have a large family and support system. Getting your cap and gown pictures, sending out invitations; planning graduation get-togethers and parties can be fun but it can engulf you. With that in mind, it's helpful if you use a digital calendar and planner to help keep you on task. Whatever your declared major is will be the department where you will get guidance on how to navigate these processes.

If you want to have your graduation event at a local venue, be sure to book in advance. Coordinate these duties with your family and friends because you really won't have the time to do this. You'll be focused on exams, papers, finals, etc. Make your graduation memorable. You've done the hard work, now it's time to celebrate the fruits of your labor.

CHAPTER 10

Your First Career Interview After Graduation! Now What?!

The time has finally come that you've been waiting for. You get the call for an interview. You have applied to job after job, but you just got a call about a CAREER opportunity. A career in your major! This is one of the most exciting feelings in the world as a new graduate and this chapter is designed to increase your chances of beating the odds that are against you. As a former HR Manager who was responsible for interviewing and hiring employees, I saw one too many new graduates that missed the basic steps that could have gotten them hired. The first thing you need to embrace is that you have an interview. There is something about you that is interesting and compelling to this potential employer. You completed the application, you submitted your resume and the recruiter was impressed enough to call you in. That's the first hurdle to jump through of the job-hunt process because depending on the industry you're in, there can be well over hundreds of resumes that are submitted. There are resumes from candidates that have similar degrees and experiences as you. There are some that have way more experience than you, and even some that will have no idea what they applied for. They just saw the salary and decided to give it a try. After weeding through all of those resumes with tracking systems that identify key words in your resume, your resume came through all of that. This means that your resume went through a competitive route in order to make it to the top for an interview. This is why you MUST bring your A-game to the first interview because there will be other candidates interviewing that will be just as eager and hungry as you are, if not more. This is the time to set the bar extremely high, making it near impossible for them to go with another candidate. This list isn't all-inclusive but it's the very core things you will need to know:

- Bring at least 3-4 copies of your resume with you on your interview. Some interviews comprise of panels and while they may have your resume on hand, it's best to assume they don't or if you've made any changes since your last resume was submitted, you'll want to have them. This is vitally important because a lot of the team's interview questions will be generated based on your resume.

- Print on resume paper. Using a high quality of paper to print your resumes demonstrates that you made an investment and believes in putting your best foot forward.

- Have a professional folder that holds all of your paperwork. A black or brown portfolio will be ideal.

- Adhere to the traditional standards of interview attire. Stick to the standard colors of black, navy, and/or gray. For women, you should have a nice skirt and blouse set, pant set, or dress that fits appropriately. The same for men. Adhere to the same colors and be sure to be properly fitted if you decide to wear a suit jacket and slacks. This is a deal-breaker for a lot of employers when a potential candidate comes in to an interview. If you're not presentable, this can backfire majorly.

- Stay away from bold hairstyles and colors. An acronym that I've revamped that help students and adults out in life is to K.I.S.S.-

Keep It Simple "Suga". Don't overthink it but just keep it simple.

- If you have tattoos that are visible, use a concealer and yes, this goes for guys too. Although some sectors of the workforce are more progressive and may be more accepting of non-traditional styles, most are still more traditional.

- Take a bath and brush your teeth. I know this may sound absurd but trust me, I've seen and experienced it all. You'd be surprised at how laxed people can be in this department.

- Work on your speaking and interviewing skills. By now, you should have watched every YouTube video under the sun on how to interview and top interview questions that most employers are going to ask. If you haven't, you should start.

- No gum chewing. Go figure.

- Leave behind the strong smelling perfumes and colognes. What smells good to you could be sickening to your interviewer.

- Make sure you're well groomed and manicured.

- Leave your cell phone behind. I literally sat on an interview in which the candidate's phone was ringing in their bag. Guess what? They didn't make it to the next round of interviews.

- Develop your handshaking skills. A firm handshake is always a plus.

- Make sure you do your homework on the company or organization you're interviewing with. You should know everything about them from their leadership team, what they do; all the way to past awards, accolades, and projects they've received. It's nothing more embarrassing than being on an interview and not having a clue about some of the basic information on the company or organization.

- Be prepared to complete a written exercise or some type of on-the spot performance that will measure your ability to think on your toes and operate under pressure.

- Be cordial and professional with everyone from the time you walk in the door and the time that you walk out. Speak to, and acknowledge, the front desk administration and have a polite demeanor towards those that may walk by. Believe me, there could be someone that has influence that can put an unexpected word in on your behalf.

- Try to remember names when introduced. I know this is a challenge for me because I'm focused on presentation and not saying anything weird. Names can sometimes escape you but if possible, focus on the Hiring

Authority and whoever you will report to if hired.

- Go in, be confident, kick ass, and land the job!

- Purchase a Hallmark card and sign with a simple and courteous "Thank You for the opportunity to interview for the role of..." Hand this card over at the end of your interview to whoever escorts you to the exit.

CHAPTER 11

Living Your Best Life? You Already Are!

You did it! You made it across the finish line and you are ready to live "your best life" right? Well, this is completely possible when you take intentional steps to creating a life of balance and discipline, and still be able to live how you want. The first thing that a lot of graduate do once they get their first major job is to make major purchases. There's nothing wrong with this but I encourage balance. Don't throw your entire earnings away on the material things but use a savings approach. Plan for big-ticket items. Develop the mindset and practice of saving more than you spend and when you spend, have a budget that is able to carry you through any potential emergencies that could arise. These are a few universal tools that you can add to your toolbox for living your best life:

- Be a cheerful giver. A universal principle known as reaping and sowing is, as matter of fact, as the law of gravity. Giving opens the door for more to come into your life. Most successful individuals generally give 10% of their earnings. I say cheerful because giving grudgingly really defeats the purpose. Being a blessing to others creates so much positive energy and power, and doing it with a heart that's not in it is like eating food just because it keeps you alive but not because you enjoy the taste of it.

- Do not be ashamed to shop for discounts and bargains. There are some things that really can be bought at a lower cost and some things will require an investment. In my experience, there are some items/things that I have to invest money in just because I know the value of longevity in some items.

- Save more than you spend. You don't have to buy EVERYTHING just because you may have the means to do so. Live below your means. Splurge a little at times to reward your hard work.

- Make intentional investments in a financial market. The best time to be aggressive with investments is during your youthful years. As we age, we tend to become more conservative and not as big of risk-takers. You're never too young to begin saving for retirement.

- NEVER loan money. If you do, have a legal professional to draw up a contract to sign. Never loan out any amount that you cannot afford to lose. I'm speaking from personal experience in the tune of $5k. This loan was made to a former friend and I had to take them to court in order to get some of the money back. If someone asks for a loan over $50, they should go to a bank.

- Look after your parents. They supported you as much as they possibly could and it's always great to do nice things for them.

- Be nice. Check preconceived notions at the door and don't allow biasness to dictate how you treat mankind.

- Develop balance as much as possible. Let loose a little. Don't be so uptight and afraid to live your best life.

- Care for others or something outside of yourself.

- Laugh often.

- Communicate with your circle as much as possible. You don't realize the value of them until they're no longer present with you.

- Avoid toxic people and relationships. Cut it off as soon as you identify it. If it's hard to cut them off, address the toxic behavior and demand change. If not, let it go. Toxic people and situations will drain the energy out of you.

- Apologize when you're in the wrong. Don't allow pride to get in the way.

- Live fearlessly but responsibly. Take chances.

- Invest in therapy and coaching. This does not mean something is wrong with you. Therapy and coaching is just like paying for a gym membership. Keeping your physical and mental health in good shape is important.

- Keep it real.

- Live life with no regrets. It's your life. Live it how you want. Only you have to contend with the choices you make.

- Love and forgive. Unforgiveness holds you back. Not the person who wronged you.

- Try something out of your comfort zone as often as possible. This will keep you sharp.

- Remember that failure is not a bad thing. Most successful people have failed at some point. The objective is to get back up and do it again, and do it even better.

- Pay your debt and whatever you may owe to family, friends, or neighbors.

- Travel. Go outside of your city, state, county, and country. You'll have a different respect and appreciation for life and humankind.

- Last, but definitely not least, enjoy every moment of your college years. Take your own personal life peaks and valleys to inspire the next 1st Generation student or the next student in your family that wants to be just like you when they grow up!

Scholarships.com Links

- **About Us**: A brief history of Scholarships.com and what we offer our users as well as partners.
- **College Scholarships**: A basic breakdown of our scholarship information.
- **College Search**: Search tuition costs, application fees and degrees offered at more than 7,000 U.S. colleges and universities.
- **Educator Resources**: Valuable information and free Scholarships.com materials.
- **Financial Aid**: From college cost calculators to aid timelines to student loans, we've got the skinny on private and federal offerings here.
- **Grants**: The scholarship's kin and the money they offer at every grade level.
- **Scholarships by Major**: An ever-growing list of major-specific awards.

- **Scholarship Search**: Create a free profile and experience our site just like our users.
- **Scholarships by Type**: Nearly 50 different categories of scholarships on our site.
- **Success Stories**: Testimonials from real scholarship winners; see the impact your award could have!

Acknowledgments

I want to acknowledge God, my Higher Power, my parents, friends, doubters, lovers, and many more for giving me the energy and inspiration to write this guide for 1st Generation college students and their parents. My road to college was rocky because I didn't have a clue of what to do or what to expect. With limited knowledge and limited resources, I had to learn a lot of things the hard and expensive way. I vowed that I would pour everything I gained into the lives of students like you who will be the first ones in your family to attend college. With confidence, fear, resilience, faith, and lots of prayer, I not only made it through undergrad, but I went on to obtain my graduate degree! I have been extremely fortunate to use my downfalls, slip ups, and "oopps" moments to bring hope and encouragement to high school students, college students, and their parents. As I continue on this journey, I hope to continue my desire and willingness to share my experiences with the world. Coming to a high school and college near you!!! Now What?!

Made in the USA
Columbia, SC
05 March 2020